LEGACY'S UNIQUE WORLD

Written by
LEGACY S. GODFREY & NANDY SMITH

Illustrated by
RÉKA KÁRPÁT

To Legacy,
my beautiful, smart, and talented daughter.
Continue to inspire the world with your life.
I am beyond grateful and proud of you!

Love always,
Mommy

Copyright © 2023 by Legacy S. Godfrey & Nandy Smith
All rights reserved. No part of this publication may be reproduced, distributed, or transmitted in any form or by any means, including photocopying, recording, or other electronic or mechanical methods, without the prior written permission of the publisher, except in the case of brief quotations embodied in critical reviews and certain other noncommercial uses permitted by copyright law. For permission requests, contact the author (nandyspeaks@gmail.com).

Hardcover ISBN: 979-8-218-29554-7
Paperback ISBN: 979-8-8689-5620-1
Library of Congress Cataloging-in-Publication Data
Library of Congress Control Number: 1-12893068591
Printed in the United States of America
First printing edition 2023.
Illustrations by DeveoStudio.com

LEGACY'S UNIQUE WORLD

Written by
LEGACY S. GODFREY & NANDY SMITH

Illustrated by
RÉKA KÁRPÁT

Hi, my name is Legacy.

I see the world in a unique way.

I am autistic so my brain works a little differently.

My parents love me very much, and they understand that I need different things to feel comfortable.

They let me have my own space to play and create, and they always listen to me when I want to talk.

But I can do more every day and I am discovering new things at school and home.

Being autistic comes with a few challenges, too. Sometimes, things that other people find easy or fun can be overwhelming or confusing for me.

But I'm lucky to have cousins who are my best friends and are happy to help me.

My cousins know that I see the world differently, and they celebrate that!

We have our own inside jokes and games that we play together.

They know just what to do when I'm feeling overwhelmed or need a break, handing me a weighted blanket or holding my hand and singing.

Being autistic is a big part of who I am,
but it's not the only important thing about me.

I'm also an artist, a reader, and a friend.

I am proud of the special way I experience the world, and I'm excited to share it with others.

Thanks for reading about
my unique world!

www.ingramcontent.com/pod-product-compliance
Lightning Source LLC
Chambersburg PA
CBHW050849010526
44107CB00017BA/1223